A Trogen Surprise

Level 9 – Gold

Helpful Hints for Reading at Home

The graphemes (written letters) and phonemes (units of sound) used throughout this series are aligned with Letters and Sounds. This offers a consistent approach to learning whether reading at home or in the classroom.

HERE ARE SOME COMMON WORDS THAT YOUR CHILD MIGHT FIND TRICKY:

water	where	would	know	thought	through	couldn't
laughed	eyes	once	we're	school	can't	our

TOP TIPS FOR HELPING YOUR CHILD TO READ:

- Encourage your child to read aloud as well as silently to themselves.
- Allow your child time to absorb the text and make comments.
- Ask simple questions about the text to assess understanding.
- Encourage your child to clarify the meaning of new vocabulary.

This book focuses on developing independence, fluency and comprehension. It is a gold level 9 book band.

A Trogen Surprise

Written by
Charis Mather

Illustrated by
Drue Rintoul

Everyone in the care home gathered around Mr Trogen to get a peek at the story in the morning's newspaper.
"Go on, read it to us, Mr Trogen," they said.

Mr Trogen found the page he was looking for. "Here it is," he said. "The Troyville Art Competition is here once again. Get creative – you don't want to miss out on the grand prize."

Everyone was very pleased about this, especially Mr Trogen. The art competition was the highlight of the year.

"Just a minute," Wilma said, putting on her glasses. "There's more."

Everyone leaned in closer. In small letters at the bottom it said:

Past winners may not join the competition this year.

"That can't be right," said Mr Trogen. "I won last year. This is my favourite event!"

"Oh well," said Albert. "You'll just have to watch, I suppose."

"That's not very kind, Albert," said Wilma.

Albert laughed. "I'll be first place this year, just you wait."

Gertrude shuffled round to pat Mr Trogen on the back. "I'm sorry, Mr Trogen. I know how much you were looking forward to the competition."
Mr Trogen was glum.

Mr Trogen went back to his room. He spotted Albert in the garden, talking on the phone.
Mr Trogen opened the window to listen in.

"I always get second place, so I got the judges to change the rules," Albert said to the person on the phone. "Now Mr Trogen won't win. He's the best artist here, you know."

Mr Trogen couldn't believe it. Albert was the reason that he couldn't join this year! He listened again.

"And just to make sure, I'm going to ruin all the other art before the contest. Then, my art has to win."

"How awful!" Mr Trogen said to himself. "He won't win if I have anything to say about it." Mr Trogen decided then that he would work on a secret art project for the competition that would ruin Albert's horrible plan.

That afternoon, Mr Trogen rounded up his friends for a secret meeting in the janitor's cupboard. He told them all about Albert and about his own plan to stop him.

"Don't worry, Mr Trogen," whispered Darren. "We'll make sure Albert doesn't find out about your art. No one will know that you're making an entry for the contest."

Weeks later, Mr Trogen finally finished his secret project. It was time for another janitor's cupboard meeting. Everyone piled in.

"Tomorrow is the competition," Mr Trogen whispered to his friends. "If we're going to catch Albert before he destroys everyone's art, we need to move the statue tonight. No one can find out."

"I can drive, but I haven't got keys for the van," said Wilma.

"I can get the keys," Darren said.

"I'll help Mr Trogen wrap the statue for the trip," Gertrude volunteered. "If it breaks, then our plan is ruined."

Gertrude and Mr Trogen got to work. They carefully wrapped the statue with Gertrude's softest knitted jumpers, hats and scarves.

Mr Trogen suddenly stopped. "I can hear someone coming," he said. "That's Albert's whistling. He's going to see the statue!"

Just in time, Gertrude leapt onto a chair, holding up one of her quilts so that it hid the whole statue. Albert was right there.

"Gertrude, what are you doing on a chair?" Albert asked.
"I'm showing Mr Trogen my favourite quilt," said Gertrude quickly.
"Hmmph," said Albert, as he carried on.
"Phew. That was close," Mr Trogen sighed.
"Good thinking!"

Meanwhile, Darren and Wilma looked for the van keys. Wilma spotted them hanging from a keyring on the doorman's belt.

"How are you going to get those?" Wilma asked Darren. "He'll definitely notice." "Don't worry," he said. "I used to be a magician. I can make anything disappear."

Wilma peeked out from their hiding spot as Darren snuck closer to the doorman. When the doorman wasn't looking, Darren carefully hooked the keyring with the end of his cane. Bit by bit, Darren pulled the cane back with the stolen van keys.

"Bravo!" Wilma whispered, as Darren gave a magician's bow.

When everyone was ready, they all helped load the statue into the van. It was time to get the art in place.

"Good luck!" said Gertrude and Darren, waving goodbye to their friends.

Wilma twisted the keys to start the van and drove off as everyone in the care home was asleep for the night.

Once they arrived at the building where the contest would be, Wilma and Mr Trogen had to unload the statue by themselves. It was hard to see exactly where they were going, but eventually they got it just where they wanted.

The next morning, everyone was getting ready for the trip to the art competition. Albert noticed that Mr Trogen was not with them.

"Where is Mr Trogen?" he asked. "Is he sulking because he knows I will win today?"

Gertrude just smiled.

At the competition, a strange present waited by the door. It was the secret statue that Mr Trogen and his friends had moved in the night. A note on the front said:

Please enjoy my entry to the competition. From, a mystery artist.

"How exciting! I wonder who it's from," said the competition judge. "Let's bring it inside."

The heavy statue was carried inside and placed in the room next to all the other art.

As the judge unwrapped the statue, Albert got more and more nervous. He could hear people behind him saying that this statue was even better than his art.

When Albert was sure that no one was looking at the new statue, he took a hammer out from his bag and started tapping away. The statue cracked a little bit. He tapped again. Some of the statue crumbled onto the floor.

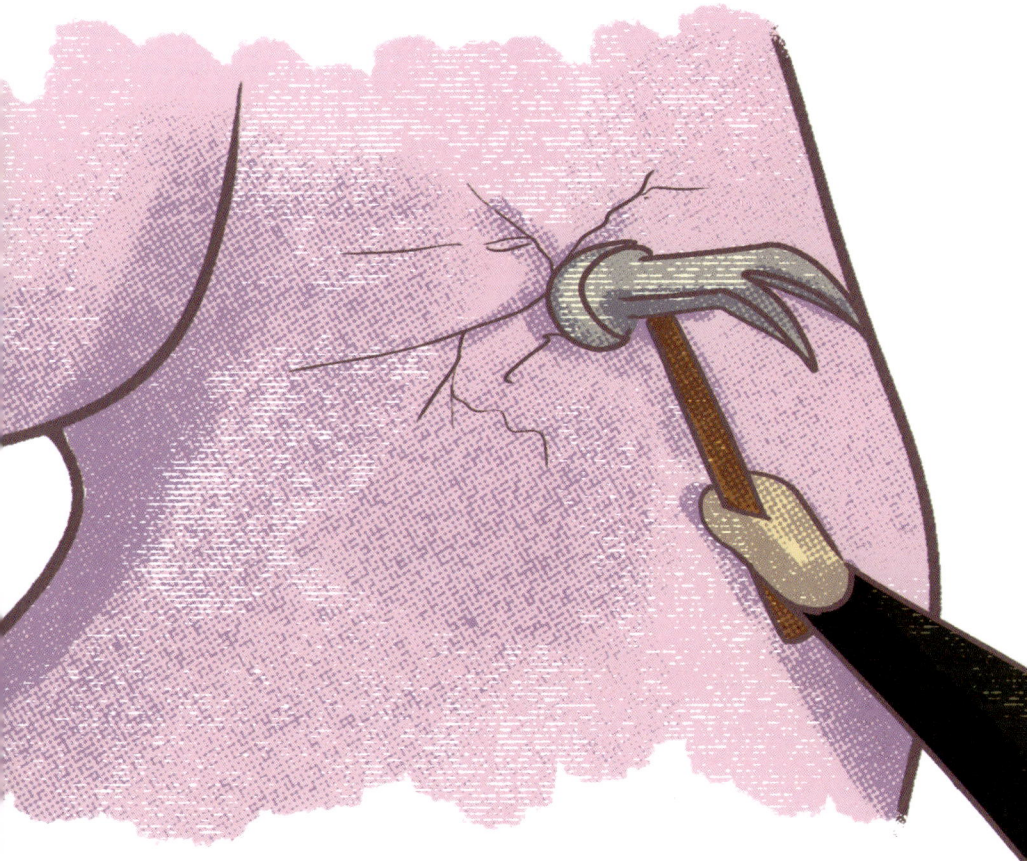

Albert laughed quietly to himself. "That's perfect. Now for the next one."

Suddenly, a loud CRACK came from the statue. Everyone jumped and looked over as the statue exploded with bits of plaster.

"Surprise!" shouted Mr Trogen as he leapt out of his statue, covered in dust. "I've caught you red-handed."

The judge hurried over. "What is going on?" he said. "Where did the statue go? And where did you come from?"

Mr Trogen was smiling ear to ear. "Mr Albert was just about to destroy everyone's art," he told the judge. "I've been hiding inside my statue all night, waiting to catch him."

Everyone gasped.
"Is this true?" the judge asked.

Albert looked at the floor, guilty. "I just didn't want to come in second place again. That's why I made it so Mr Trogen couldn't join in this year. The statue was going to win if I didn't break it."

"Well," said the judge. "You won't be winning the Troyville Art Competition this year. You're out of the competition for cheating. Let's clean up this mess and decide on the real winner."

Albert felt terrible. Not only was he not first place – he was not even in the competition at all.

The judge left to look at the rest of the art. Albert went up to Mr Trogen, who was brushing plaster off his clothes.

"I'm sorry for breaking your statue, Mr Trogen. I was jealous. And I'm sorry for trying to keep you out of the competition," said Albert. "It's no fun when you can't join in."

Mr Trogen laughed. "My statue was supposed to break, thankfully. I'm glad you have learnt your lesson."

"Let's do it properly next year," said Albert. "We'll have a fair competition."

Mr Trogen smiled and shook Albert's hand. "I like the sound of that."

A Trogen Surprise

1. Why was Mr Trogen not allowed to enter the art competition this year?

2. What plan does Mr Trogen come up with to foil Albert's plot?

3. What does Gertrude use to hide Mr Trogen's statue from Albert?

    a) A mattress

    b) A pillow

    c) A quilt

4. How do you think Albert felt after Mr Trogen stopped his plot?

5. What does it mean to have a fair competition? Why is it important to be fair?

©2022 **BookLife Publishing Ltd.**
King's Lynn, Norfolk, PE30 4LS, UK

ISBN 978-1-80155-807-5

All rights reserved. Printed in Poland.
A catalogue record for this book is available from the British Library.

A Trogen Surprise
Written by Charis Mather
Illustrated by Drue Rintoul

An Introduction to BookLife Readers...

Our Readers have been specifically created in line with the London Institute of Education's approach to book banding and are phonetically decodable and ordered to support each phase of Letters and Sounds.

Each book has been created to provide the best possible reading and learning experience. Our aim is to share our love of books with children, providing both emerging readers and prolific page-turners with beautiful books that are guaranteed to provoke interest and learning, regardless of ability.

BOOK BAND GRADED using the Institute of Education's approach to levelling.

PHONETICALLY DECODABLE supporting each phase of Letters and Sounds.

EXERCISES AND QUESTIONS to offer reinforcement and to ascertain comprehension.

BEAUTIFULLY ILLUSTRATED to inspire and provoke engagement, providing a variety of styles for the reader to enjoy whilst reading through the series.

AUTHOR INSIGHT:
CHARIS MATHER

Charis Mather is a children's author at BookLife Publishing who has a love for writing stories. Charis enjoys both reading and writing about the weird and wonderful, whether from the real world or from the imagination. Her studies in linguistics and experiences working with young readers have given her a knack for writing material that suits a range of ages and skill levels. Charis is passionate about producing books that emphasise the fun in reading and is convinced that no matter how much you already know, there is always something new to learn.

This book focuses on developing independence, fluency and comprehension. It is a gold level 9 book band.